UNBELIEVABLE!

THE SECRETS OF MAGIC REVEALED BY
STEPHEN MULHERN

Piccadilly

First published in the UK in 2025 by
PICCADILLY PRESS
an imprint of Bonnier Books UK
5th Floor, HYLO, 105 Bunhill Row, London EC1Y 8LZ

A CIP catalogue record for this book is available from the British Library.

ISBN: 978-1-80078-385-0
Signed edition ISBN: 978-1-83587-425-7

1

Designed and Illustrated by Jeni Child
Illustrations of Max Magic, his top hat and gold coins
by Begoña Fernández Corbalán
Cover photograph and page 93 courtesy of Lifted Entertainment
Edited by Jenny Jacoby
Printed and bound in China

The authorised representative in the EEA is
Bonnier Books UK (Ireland) Limited.
Registered office address: Floor 3, Block 3,
Miesian Plaza, Dublin 2, D02 Y754, Ireland
compliance@bonnierbooks.ie

bonnierbooks.co.uk/PiccadillyPress

CONTENTS

HELLO!

It's Stephen Mulhern here, and this is my first ever book where I show you some of my favourite magic tricks and show you how to do them too.

They say magicians should never reveal their secrets. But I say, if you never reveal any secrets, how will we ever find the magicians of the future?

This is the reason I've created this book, and I promise that if you go through it and practise your favourite tricks to perform, you will become a magician too!

Prepare yourself to learn some of the best secrets of magic. In this book I start with some key techniques and then teach you some brilliant tricks, and how to make your own! Read how I got started, see some of my top tips to get yourself out of tricky situations, and end up with a brand-new hobby – or even a career that may change your life!

Thank you so much for taking the time to read my book.

Now, let the magic begin!

THE GIFT OF MAGIC

For me, being a magician is a dream. I've loved the art of magic and illusion from a very young age, and I started practising and learning it properly from the age of 11.

As a family, me and my brothers and my sister would gather around the TV to watch a master magician called Paul Daniels. He would take my breath away. People being sawn in half and then put back together again? It blew my mind, and my dad noticed. So, at the end of the night, when most parents read their kids bedtime stories, Dad started doing magic.

Night after night, he'd show us impossible tricks. In Dad's hands, coins disappeared and reappeared, cards changed their faces and teacups floated in the air – even while he poured tea into them! Unbelievable? It blew my mind too! After his bedtime shows, I'd spend half the night awake, trying to work out how he did it . . .

When my Dad realised how much I loved magic, he decided to teach me the secrets – like I am going to be doing in this book for you.

I wasn't as good at most school subjects as my friends were, but when I performed my first trick in the playground, the reaction was gold! They loved it! That gasp, that wow – it's still the best feeling ever.

Performing magic for someone else is a beautiful gift to give, no matter how old or young your audience. It's even better if they know they've helped you do it, because you've given them a chance to do magic too. That can make their whole day.

Here and now, with this book in your hands, I want to give you what my dad gave me: *the unbelievable secrets of magic.*

BANANA SPLIT

The first trick that wowed my friends at school was called the Banana Split! As soon as my dad showed me how to do it, no banana was safe from me.

YOU WILL NEED

* A banana
* A long, thin sewing pin

In this one, you'll learn to chop a banana into little round slices without even peeling it first. Set aside some time to prepare where your audience can't see you . . .

1 Poke the pin into one side of the banana, a little way up from one end. Push it through the fruit until you feel the skin on the other side, then stop so it doesn't go all the way through.

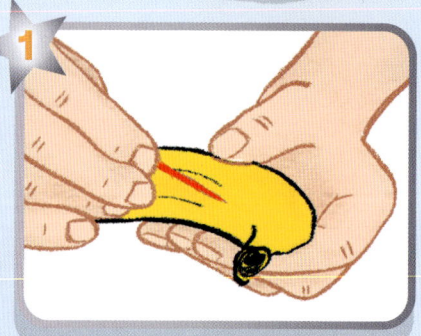

2 Keeping the hole as small as possible, wobble the pin carefully from side to side. This makes your first slice! Remove the pin.

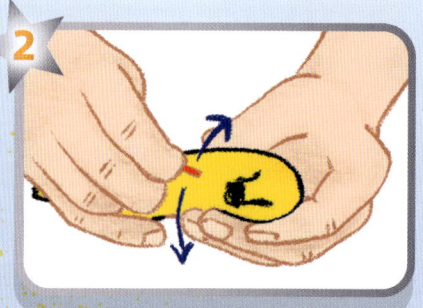

3 Repeat these steps at three or four other places along the banana.

4 Showtime! Wait for someone to take the banana, or offer it to them. Even if they inspect it, they won't notice the pinholes!

5 Ask if they know how to slice a banana without opening it.

6 When they give you the banana back, softly karate-chop it over each pin cut.

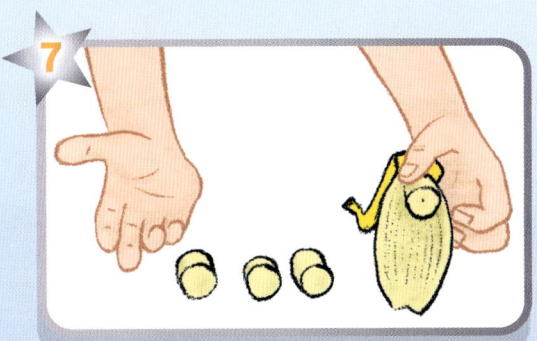

7 Offer it back for them to peel, and right where you pretended to chop it, the peeled banana will reveal five neat round slices. Incr-edible!

A ROUTINE FOR YOUR ROUTINE

Magic, like many things in life, is all about practice, personality, preparation and performance. With hard work, you can't go wrong!

There's nothing like the joy of wowing people with a trick! Unfortunately, as much as your audience love the mystery of great magic, they're desperate to catch you out! Here's the method to make your routines flawless, and take the pressure off.

PRACTICE

When you start learning a new trick, however simple or complicated, the only way you will improve is by practising. Go slowly as you perfect the moves, then repeat and repeat. Drop things. Slip up. Try again. Soon you won't even need to think!

PERSONALITY

Your audience wants to see magic, but they also want to see you! With a dash of your unique, creative personality, even old tricks will feel new for them. Look for opportunities to create fresh twists and turns, and you'll be inventing your own tricks in no time!

PREPARATION

When you're performing for other people, you never know exactly what your audience will or won't do. The job of any great magician is to be prepared for anything! Plan out a solution for every single way they could surprise you, and you'll be ready to keep the trick on track.

PERFORMANCE

You've done the practice, added your own flair and gathered an audience. Now don't forget to have fun! People can tell when you're enjoying your routines. Even when things go a bit wrong, everyone will be happy to know you're having a good time, and that will help them appreciate the whole show!

THE MAGIC OF MISTAKES

Life is unpredictable. Things go wrong. Being a magician means always thinking ahead. So if you learn to anticipate problems like a magician, you'll have fewer to deal with in all walks of life. In magic, a backup plan is called a 'get-out'. They sure come in handy!

HOW TO FIND YOUR GET-OUTS

Let's say you're on stage with a card face-down in your hand. You ask someone to think of any playing card. They choose the six of diamonds, but when you turn over the card in your hand you reveal . . . the seven of hearts! Oh dear.

This is when you need to remember that you're the ringmaster here. Take control of your audience. Make them believe that you know what you're doing – *especially* when you don't. They didn't come along expecting mistakes, which means you don't need to tell them when mistakes crop up! Trust me, they wouldn't want to know. If you have confidence, they will too. But what now?

You could make fun of the mistake by pretending it was a deliberate joke, and while they're laughing, you're planning. For certain tricks, you can use that new information to fix it: they've just seen you break the rules, and you'll still get away with it!

For example, now you know they want the six of diamonds. While they're laughing at your obvious joke, use a different skill to find the six and hide it – maybe up your sleeve, or perhaps behind the wrong one. 'Oh, unbelievable! These new cards are misbehaving. Let's see now, if I rub it on my sleeve . . . There we go! Our lazy six of diamonds, here at last!'

A mistake? Not any more. You've just found your get-out, and invented a new trick, live!

STAGE FRIGHT

When mistakes happen, it's natural to feel nervous. Your hands might shake. Your voice might wobble. Take a moment. Breathe.

You're nervous because, for you, what was *meant* to happen *didn't* happen. That's OK! Nobody else knows how it was supposed to go. If you keep your cool, they'll assume this is your unique twist. Never reveal the real plan, and they'll never know when it's gone wrong!

TRICKY BUSINESS

When you perform a trick, you get three reactions, one after the other. First, people are amazed! Second, they want to know how it's done. And third, they want to see more. To get these reactions, you need to:

1 Complete your trick perfectly

2 Entertain with your performance

3 Surprise your audience

Once you've learned how to do these three things, you will be able to perform magic on any scale: from the smallest trick to the biggest miracle!

Once you've tried all the tricks, make them your own! If you get stuck, go to page 93 for a link to a video showing some tips from Stephen!

WHAT WILL MY AUDIENCE EXPECT?

HOW CAN I SURPRISE THEM?

LEARN THE TRICK'S BASIC SKILLS

PRACTISE UNTIL PERFECT

PERFORM TO A KIND AUDIENCE

MAKE THE TRICK YOUR OWN

WHAT COULD GO WRONG?

BE CREATIVE

WHAT ARE MY GET-OUTS?

SHOWTIME

You've learned your tricks, you've practised until you can do them with your eyes shut, and you're prepared for anything that could go wrong. What else can make sure that everyone – including you – will enjoy the performance?

PROPS CHECK

Props are what magicians call any items used in a show. Before any performance - whether for your best friend or a hall of strangers - carefully check that you have all your props ready in the right places. It's better to be late than unprepared.

OUTFIT CHECK

If any of your tricks rely on hiding things in your sleeves, pockets or shoes, make sure your outfit includes those features! Some magicians dress like wizards, some dress smartly and some wear their everyday outfits. Whatever you choose, make sure that it's comfortable and practical!

PLAYING WITH PATTER

Patter is the term for what magicians say while performing. It entertains and guides the audience's attention: if you speak, they will naturally look at your face. So, quick, do something with your hands! Tell jokes, share stories, recite mystical rhymes or even chat to the front row, but let your patter reflect your personality. Remember, they're here for you!

WARMING UP

Before you go on stage, prepare yourself physically with exercises. For instance, if your tricks require talking, check you can speak in a loud and clear voice. If you're working with your hands, warm them up to be sure your fingers are nimble.

WATCH AND LEARN

If you're part of a larger show, stick around after your bit to study the other routines! When I was a kid, I would travel down to Covent Garden in London to watch the street artists and entertainers. This was a great way to get inspiration, learn from other performers and see what worked – and what didn't! I took those ideas home to improve my own performances.

WARMING UP

A lot of these tricks rely on concealing objects with just your own two hands, so they'll need warming up first! These exercises will get your fingers quick and nimble.

YOU WILL NEED

★ Two coins

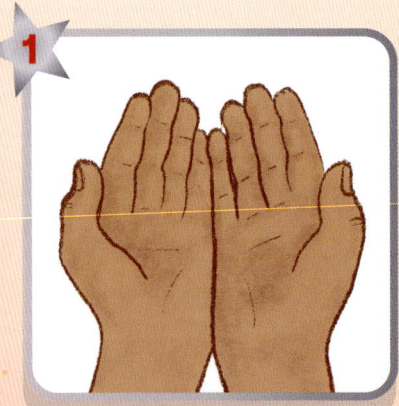

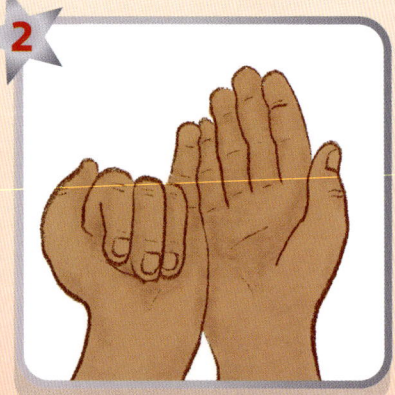

1 Hold your hands out together, palms empty and open, facing up.

2 Starting with the index finger on your left hand, bend each of your fingers into your palms and keep them there.

3

Once both hands are closed, reverse the action: starting with the index finger on your right hand, open your hands.

4

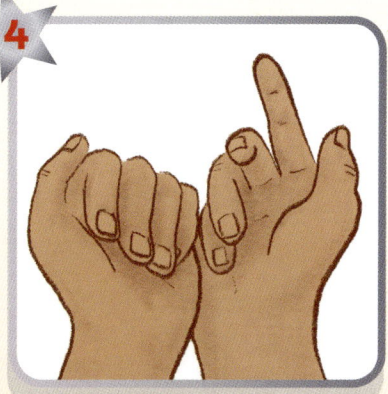

Repeat opening and closing your hands until the action is smooth, with no pauses.

5

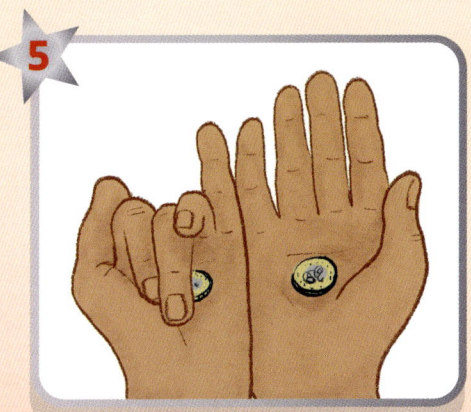

Now, place a coin in the centre of each palm – it's a little trickier! – and repeat again until your hands are warmed up for magic.

TOP TIP

Unlike most tricks, you might find this one easier with your eyes closed!

HOW TO SHUFFLE

Shuffling a deck of cards is key to many card tricks. The audience needs to see you shuffle so they know that the cards aren't rigged — so practise this riffle shuffle to really look the part before you start any magic!

YOU WILL NEED

★ A deck of playing cards

1

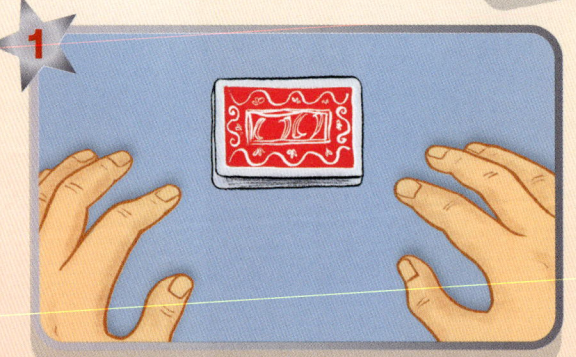

Start with the deck face-down on the table in front of you.

2

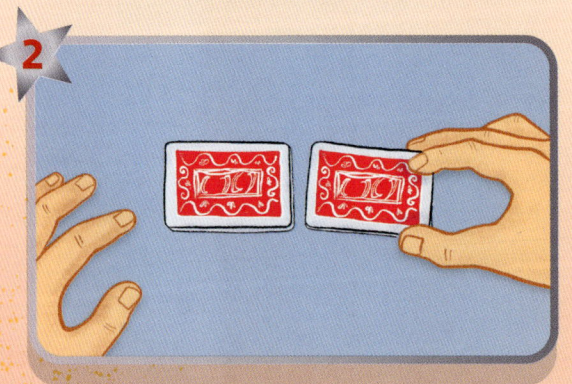

Separate the deck into two halves and place them end-to-end.

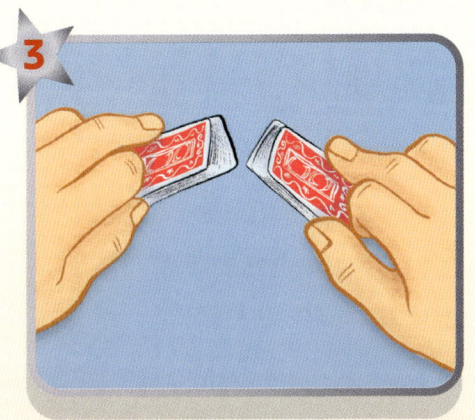

3 Grip one half in each hand, with your thumb holding the near edge, your fingers holding the far sides, and your forefinger folded and pressing down in the middle of the pile.

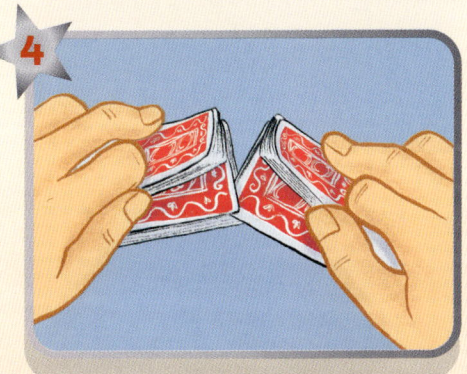

4 Holding the corner of the two piles together, slowly slide your thumbs up the edge of each pile so that one by one the cards riffle down and interweave with each other.

5 Push the piles together and neaten the edges.

When you have perfected this skill, can you try it in the air?

PALMING A COIN

Hiding a small item in your palm is known as *palming* it: an essential technique for many up-close tricks, especially coin tricks. Practise until you can do it without thinking, then substitute the coin for any other small object!

YOU WILL NEED

★ A coin

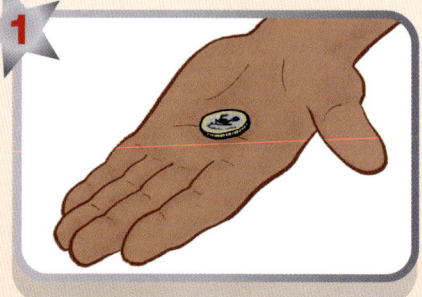

1 Place the coin in the centre of one flat, open palm.

TOP TIP

The larger the coin, the easier! To improve, use smaller and smaller coins.

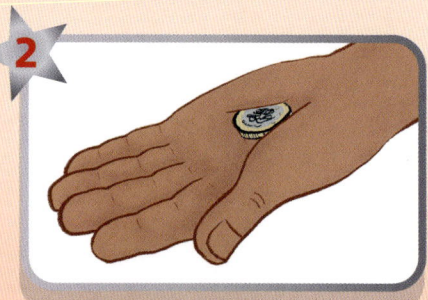

2 With the base of the same thumb, squeeze the coin, gripping it in your palm.

3

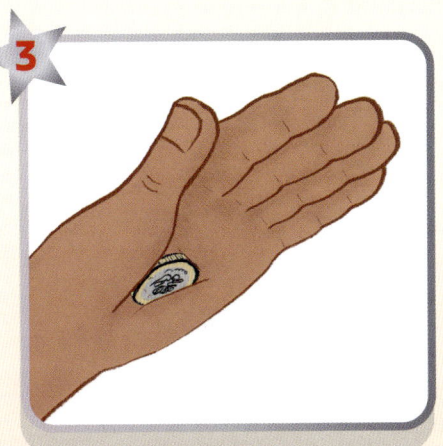

Practise turning your hand over, palm down, without the coin dropping out. Do the same with your empty hand, making them look equally relaxed and natural.

4

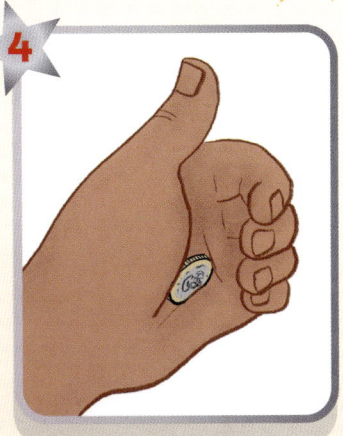

Using only your coin hand, practise pinching the coin out of your palm with your fingertips.

5

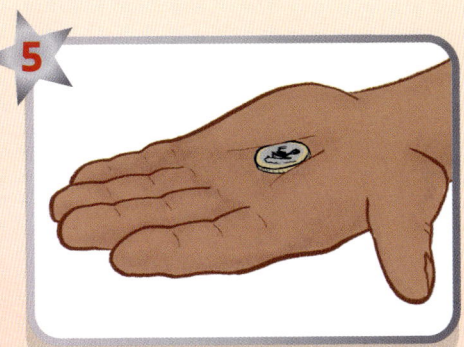

Now try to put it back!

Use this technique to pluck a coin from behind a friend's ear!

FALSE TRANSFER

This key technique convinces your audience that a coin has moved from one hand to the other, when really it stays hidden in the original hand!

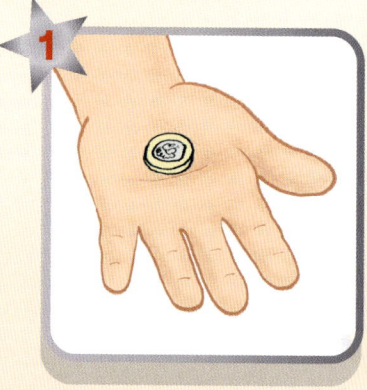

YOU WILL NEED

⭐ A coin

Show your audience a coin in the palm of your preferred hand.

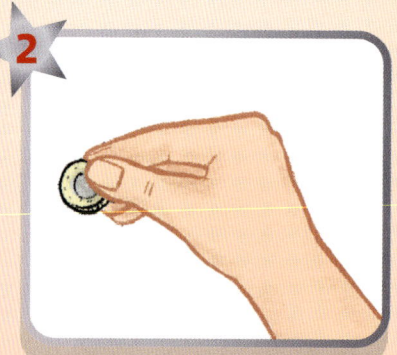

With the thumb and forefinger of the same hand, move the coin into a pinch grip. Keep your spare fingers together underneath your index finger, like a wall.

SECRET VIEW

Posing your other hand similarly, cover your coin hand from your audience.

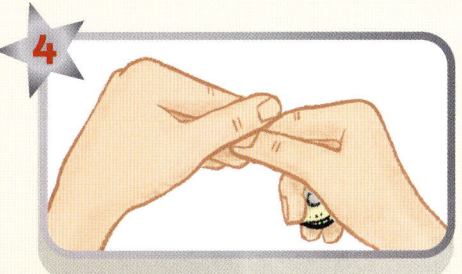

4

With the thumb of your coin hand, move the coin down to hold between your second and third fingers.

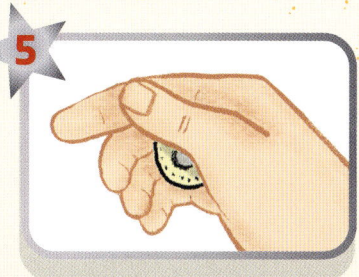

5

Curl those fingers inwards to hide the coin.

6

Make a show of closing your other hand into a fist and flourish it away, pretending that you have taken the coin out of your coin hand.

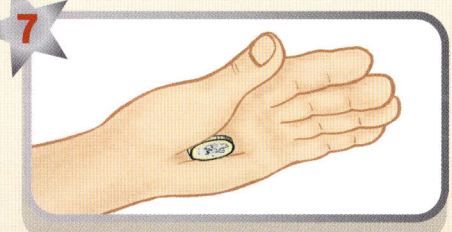

7

While the audience is distracted, casually drop your coin hand to your side and palm the coin (page 22). Relax your fingers so your hand looks empty.

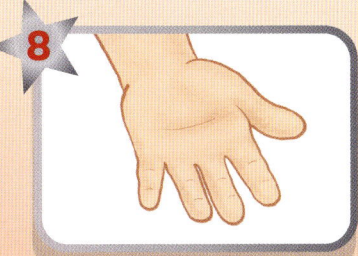

8

Open your fist to show the coin has vanished!

TOP TIP

Practise in front of a mirror, alternating between real and false transfers, to make sure they look the same.

LAPPING

Lapping is the magic word for hiding something in your lap. Once you can master the art of taking things into and out of your lap without the audience noticing, the only limit is your imagination!

YOU WILL NEED

★ A small item: a coin, a glue stick, a tape measure

SECRET VIEW

To practise, sit at a table with your thighs level and your knees together.

Place the item in your steady lap and practise moving naturally.

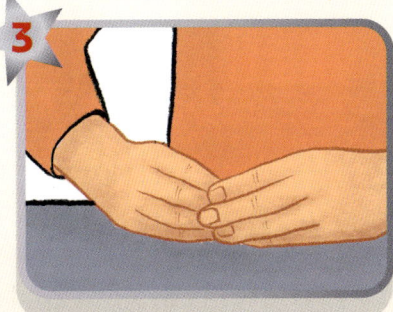

Showtime! With an audience, place the object on the edge of your table.

Making your hands a wall with your thumbs tucked out of sight, hide the object from your audience. Keeping your (and their!) attention on your hands, use your thumbs to nudge it into your lap.

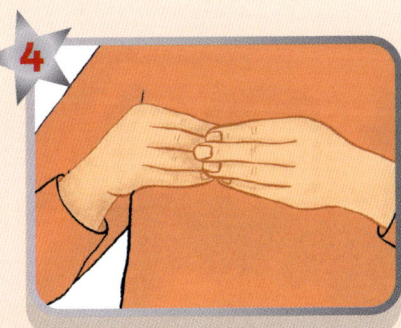

Raise your hands up as if you're levitating the object.

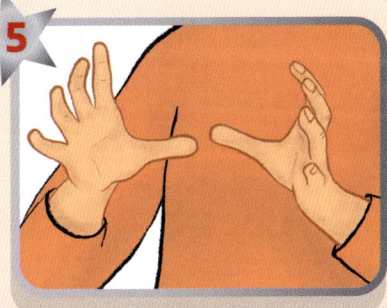

Blow on your hands and . . . Unbelievable! It's disappeared!

TOP TIP Practise with a mirror at different table heights and eye-levels!

THE MAGIC PENCIL

Using the audience's attention to hide your magic is known as *misdirection,* and it's brilliant for vanishing tricks. The idea here is that a big movement can distract your audience from a small movement.

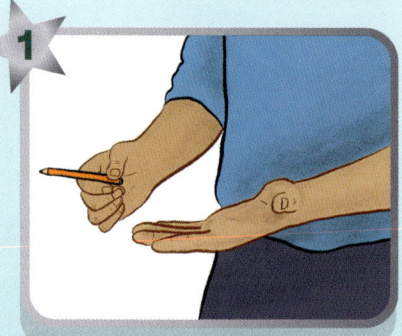

1

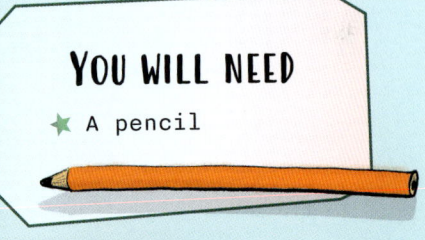

YOU WILL NEED

★ A pencil

Pinch the pencil in your preferred hand, angling this side of your body away from your audience. Hold out your other hand, palm up.

3

SECRET VIEW

2 Gesturing with the pencil, tell your audience that you will make a coin appear in your empty hand on the count of three. This is your misdirection!

Begin the countdown, raising the pencil up to your ear and bringing it down on your empty palm. Loud and clear, count 'one . . .'

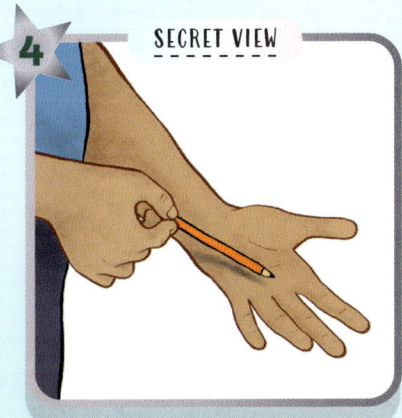

4 SECRET VIEW

Raise and lower the pencil again, while counting 'two . . .'

5 As you raise the pencil for the final count of three, tuck it behind your hidden ear!

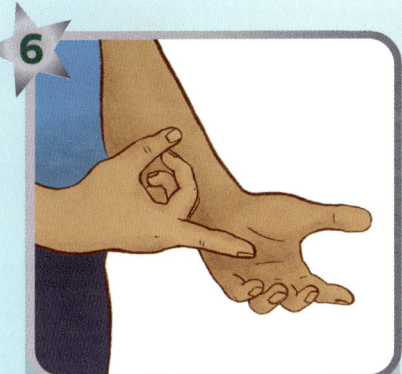

6 On the count of 'three', clap your empty hand down on your palm.

7 Showing your empty hands, exclaim that the pencil has disappeared! As for the coin: what coin?!

TOP TIP

You'll have to get the pencil off your ear eventually, so maybe let them see it as you turn or bow. Magic and a laugh!

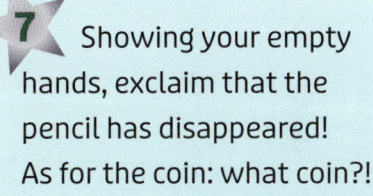

THE LOST COIN

This is an astonishing trick
to vanish a coin in your bare hands.
The secret? It never goes anywhere!
But it sure is a sticky situation . . .

YOU WILL NEED

* A coin (the lighter, the easier)
* Double-sided sticky tape

1

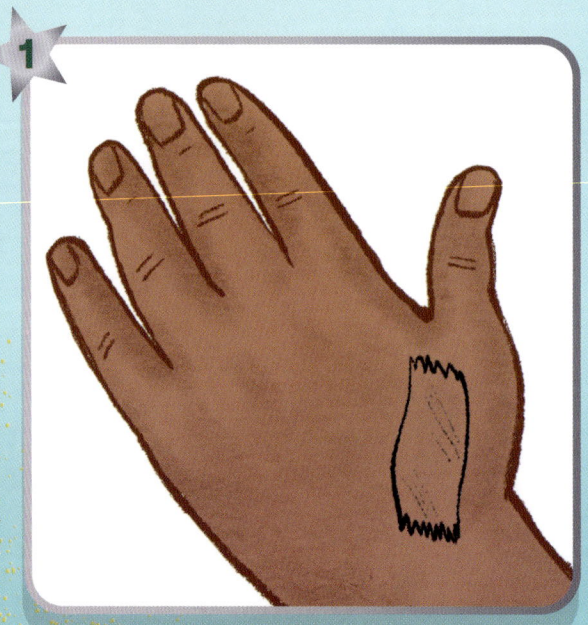

Before the show, put a strip of double-sided sticky tape on the back of your hand, between the base of your thumb and index finger.

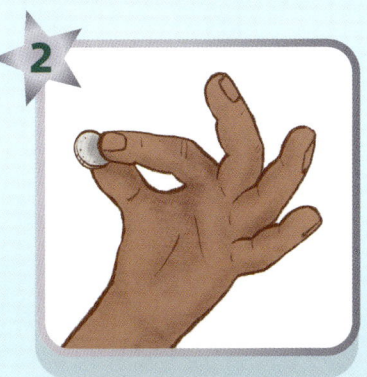

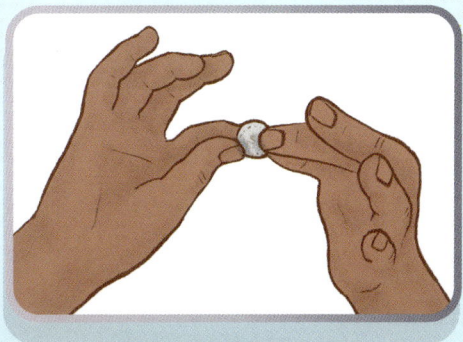

Showtime! Show the coin to your audience, passing it between your hands to build up anticipation. Keep the back of your taped hand hidden!

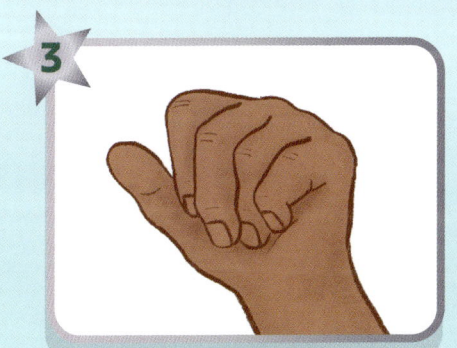

Make a fist of your taped hand, explaining that you will place the coin inside.

Pretend to push the coin into your fist, but secretly stick it to the tape.

FRONT VIEW

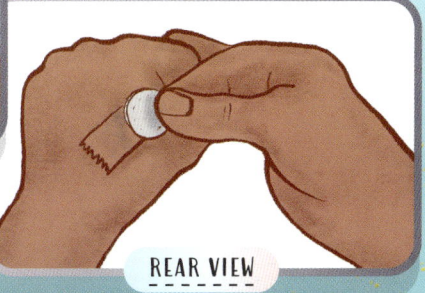

REAR VIEW

FRONT VIEW

With a magical flourish, open both hands to reveal –
nothing! Unbelievable!

REAR VIEW

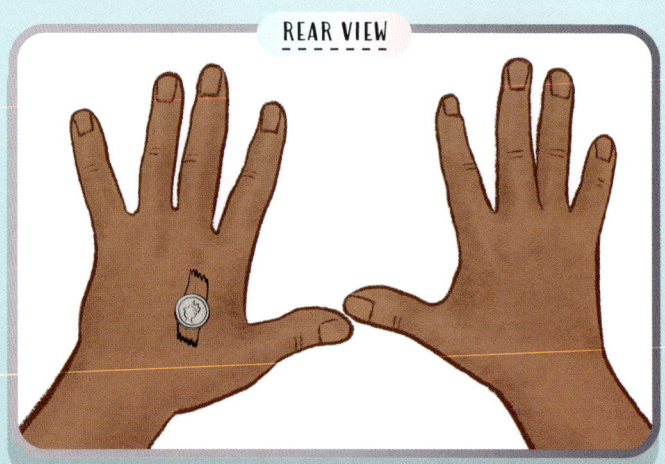

TOP TIP

The more effort you make to
poke the coin into your fist, the
more your audience will believe
you – but don't overdo it!

THE WATERFALL

How can you make water vanish without drinking it – or getting soaking wet? With a little preparation! In this trick, your audience will see and hear the water as it pours from one mug to the other . . . never to be seen again!

YOU WILL NEED

* Two mugs (not see-through)
* A small jug of water
* Kitchen roll

Before the show, fill your first mug about a quarter full with water.

2

Scrunch up a pad of kitchen roll and push it down tight into the second mug.

3 Showtime! Tell your audience that you will make the water in the first mug vanish. Feel free to show them the water in there!

4

Next, pour the water into the second mug. Make a show of it: as high as you can!

5 Show the empty mug, then put it down.

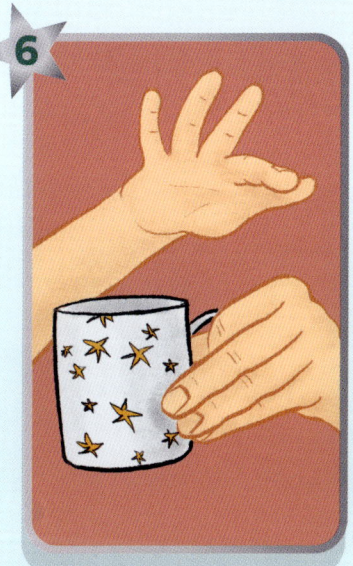

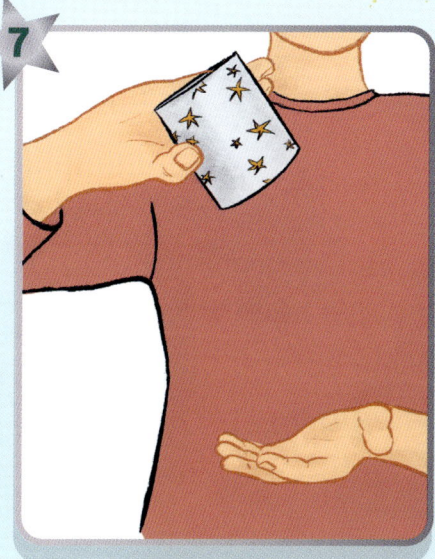

Make a magical gesture over the full mug, giving time for the water to soak into the kitchen roll.

Turning the 'full' mug towards you – so your audience can't see inside – flip the mug upside down. Not a drop spilled, so the water must be gone!

Try adding a couple of ice cubes on top of the wad of kitchen roll. Now, when you turn the mug upside down, you'll have turned the water into ice!

THE DISAPPEARING BUD

People have probably told you cotton buds aren't for your ears, and that's right: they're for magic! Your audience won't believe how quickly this cotton bud will vanish . . .

YOU WILL NEED
* A cotton bud
* Double-sided sticky tape

1

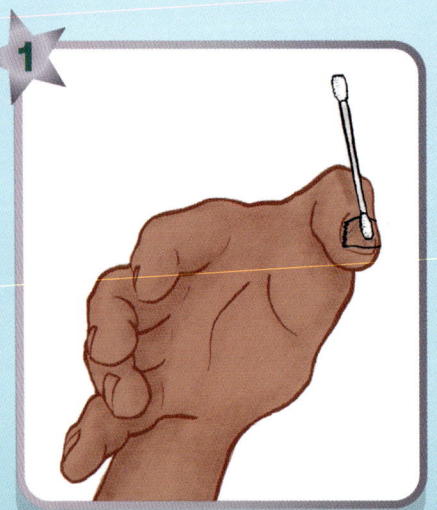

Before the show, use double-sided sticky tape to attach one end of the cotton bud to your thumbnail.

2

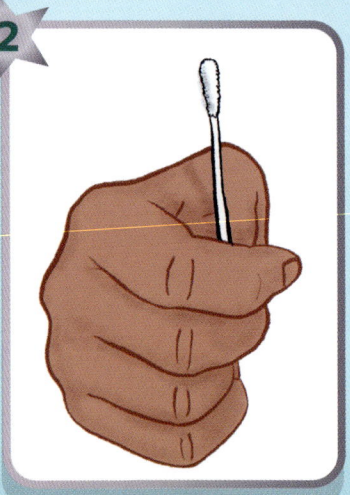

Showtime! Show your audience the cotton bud by closing your thumb into your fist.

3 Tell your audience you will make it disappear, and then simply . . .

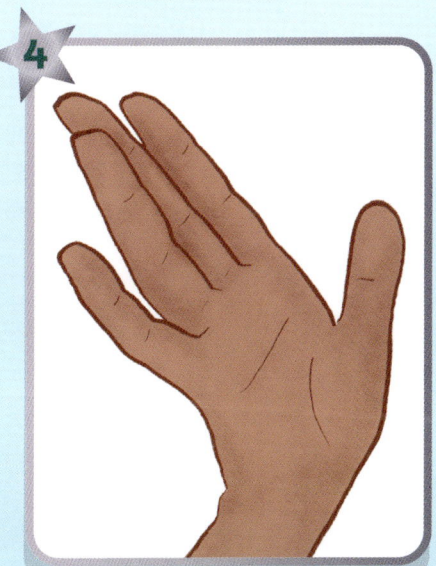

4

Open your hand!

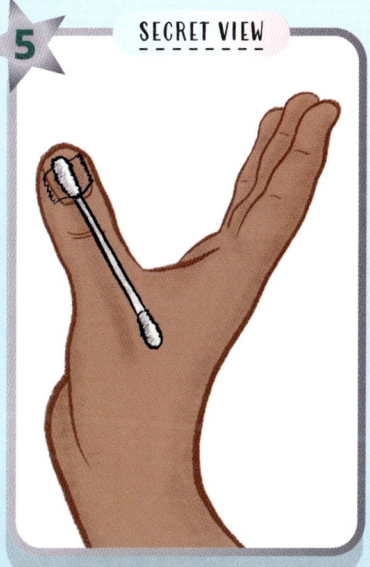

5 SECRET VIEW

The cotton bud will fly back behind your thumb where the audience can't see it.

TOP TIP

While they react, wave your hands around to disguise taking it off the tape!

Pockets are useful for hiding the bud after the trick!

THE VANISHING PEN

You've never seen a pen move this fast! This disappearing pen trick is a great one to have *up your sleeve* . . . Still, it takes a little tinkering to set up in advance.

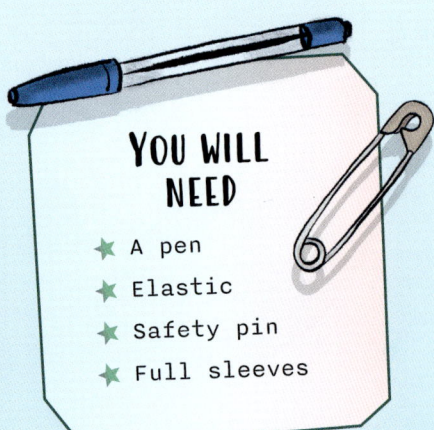

YOU WILL NEED

* A pen
* Elastic
* Safety pin
* Full sleeves

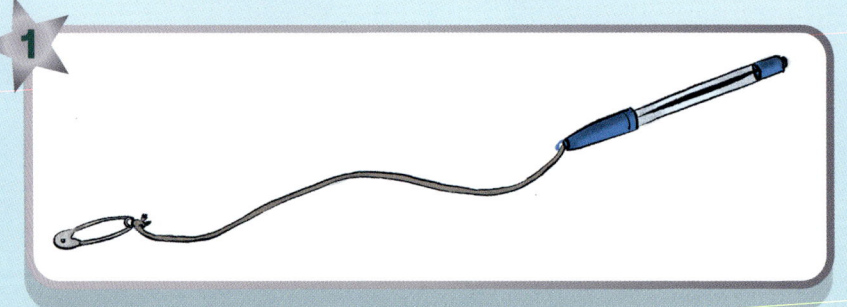

1

Cut a piece of elastic about 30cm long. Tie one end to the safety pin loop and the other end to the pen lid.

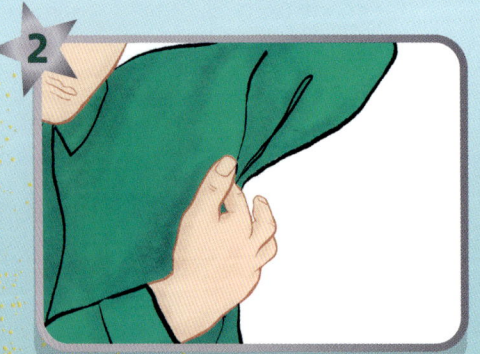

2

Attach the safety pin to the armpit inside of your sleeve, and run the elastic down. The pen should hang, unseen, inside your sleeve.

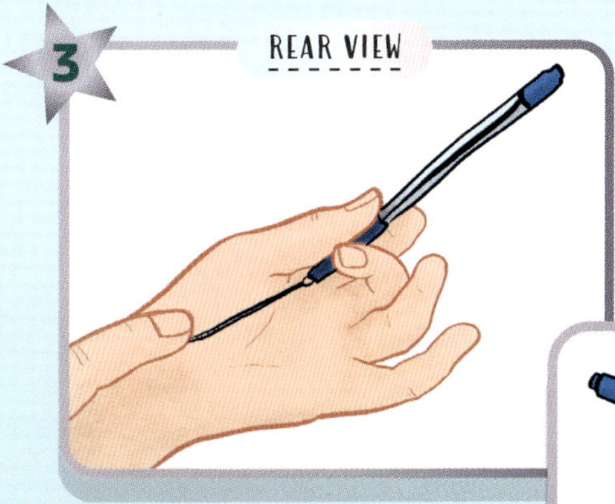

REAR VIEW

During the show, pull the pen down into your hand. Display the pen with the elastic hidden.

FRONT VIEW

'Now you see it ...'

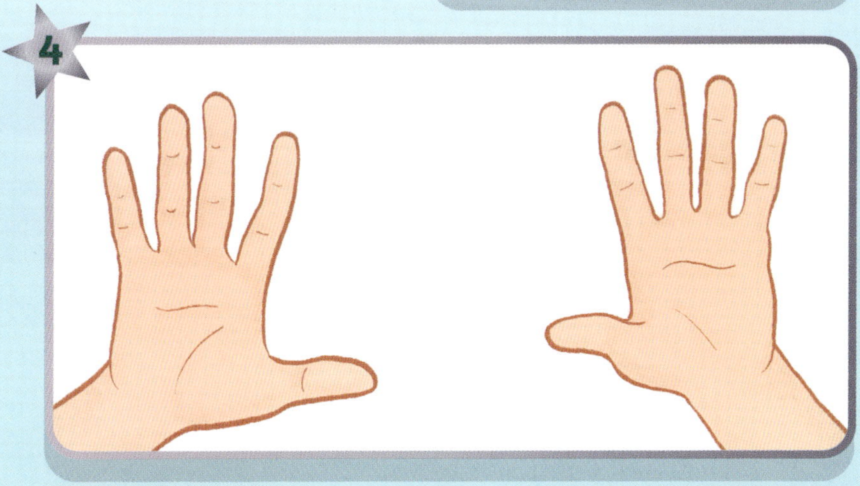

4

Let go of the pen, whizzing it up your sleeve.

'And now you don't!'

TOP TIP For extra pizzazz and misdirection as you vanish the pen, click your fingers with the other hand!

THE MAGIC PAPER WALLET

In this trick, you fold a piece of paper
around a coin to trap it in a wallet,
then rip up the paper to reveal — no coin!
Money can be like that sometimes . . .

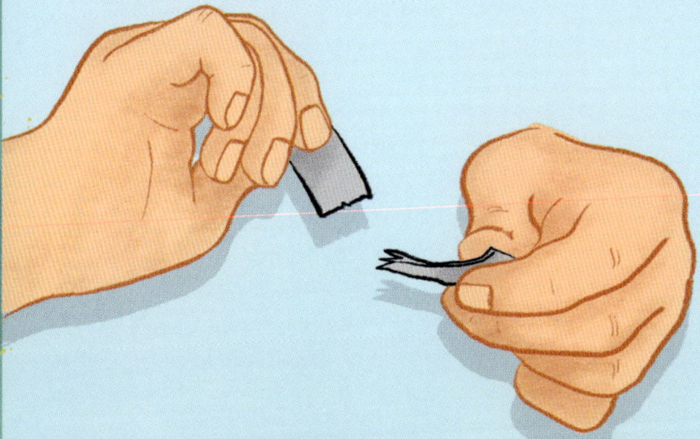

YOU WILL NEED

- A coin
- A square piece of paper

1

Fold a square piece of
paper into nine squares.

2

Place the coin in the middle.

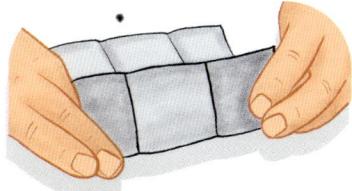

a. Fold the top third down over the coin

b. Keeping the coin where it is, turn it all over

c. Fold the left section in

d. Fold the right section in

e. Fold the bottom up to the middle

4

Pressing the coin, hold the envelope up to show the audience its outline.

5 SECRET VIEW

SECRET VIEW

Loosen your grip just enough to let the coin fall into your hand and palm it.

6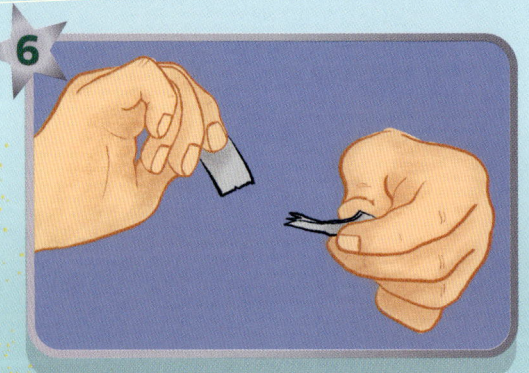

With both hands, tear up the paper!

TOP TIP

While they're amazed, get rid of the coin . . .

SPONGE SQUARES

This is one of my favourites! It involves taking two sponge squares and making one vanish from your pocket to reappear in someone else's hand. This one's got audience participation!

YOU WILL NEED

* Three palm-sized sponge squares
* Clothes with pockets

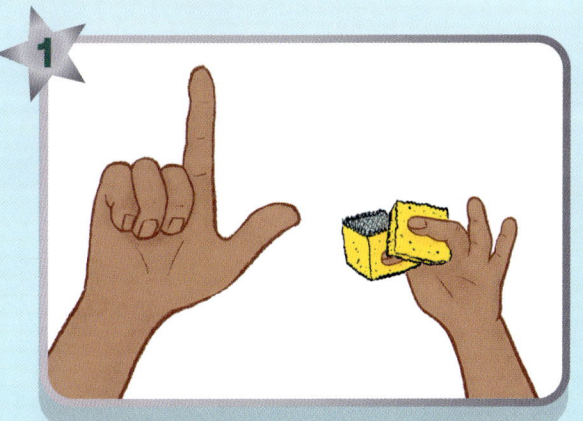

1

Without your audience seeing, hide one sponge in your hand, leaving the index finger and thumb free.

2

Showtime! Hold one square visibly in each hand, both in the same position.

3

Ask an audience member to come forward and hold out their hand for a sponge.

4

Using the two-sponge hand, press them both into the audience member's hand.

5

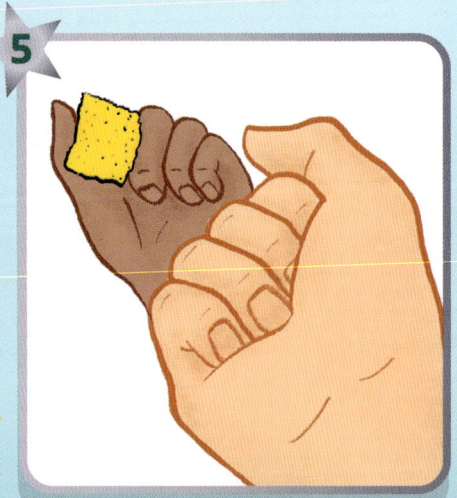

Tell your volunteer to squeeze 'the sponge' tightly. They'll think they're only holding one!

6

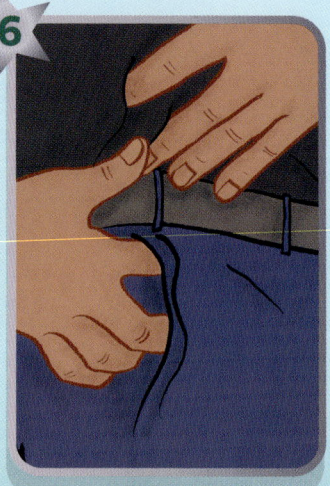

Make a show of putting the third sponge into your pocket – but push it down tight.

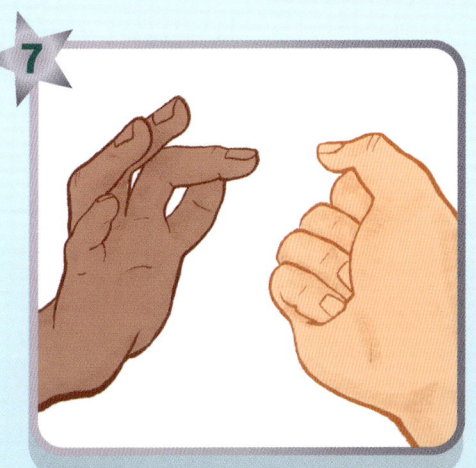

7

Tap your pocket. Tap the volunteer's hand. Do a magical gesture.

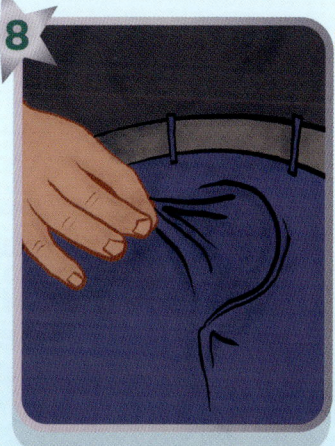

8

Turn out your pocket enough to look empty (keeping the sponge safely tucked away).

9

Ask your volunteer to open their hand . . . and two sponges fly out!

TOP TIP

If you aren't wearing anything with pockets, mix it up with a new hiding place, like under your arm or in the toe of your shoe!

THE LIPSTICK SHIFT

Magicians know their way around make-up: it's another kind of magic! In this trick, you shift a lipstick mark around someone's hand, from the back to the palm. A bold-coloured lipstick works best — but if you borrow one, ask first!

YOU WILL NEED

★ A lipstick (get permission first!)

1

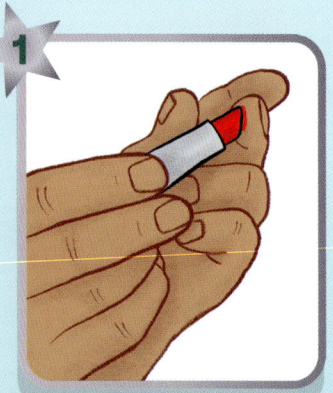

2

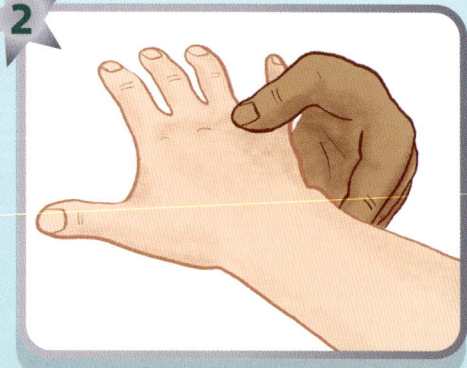

Before the show, dab colourful lipstick onto the pad of your middle finger.

Ask a volunteer to stick their hand out. Use your hand to adjust it to a different height and, at the same time, secretly dab your painted finger on their palm. Misdirection!

3

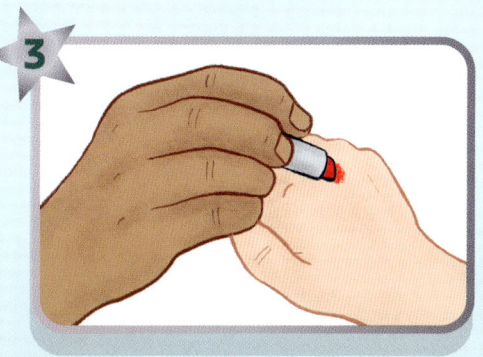

Have them make a tight fist, then dab the tube of lipstick on the back of their hand.

4

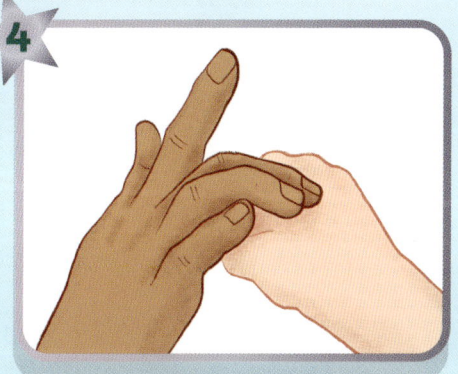

Rub the lipstick in, as if sending the colour through their hand! This now explains why you have a dab on your finger.

5

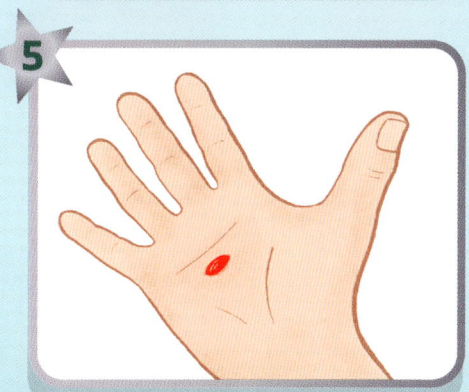

Ask them to reveal their palm. The colour has shifted through!

TOP TIP

To protect the illusion, keep the lipstick marks roughly the same size.

THE TWIN COINS

In the blink of an eye, a coin jumps from one hand to the other, reuniting with its friend! This trick is a great place to learn sleight-of-hand skills that are vital for advanced magic.

YOU WILL NEED
★ Two coins

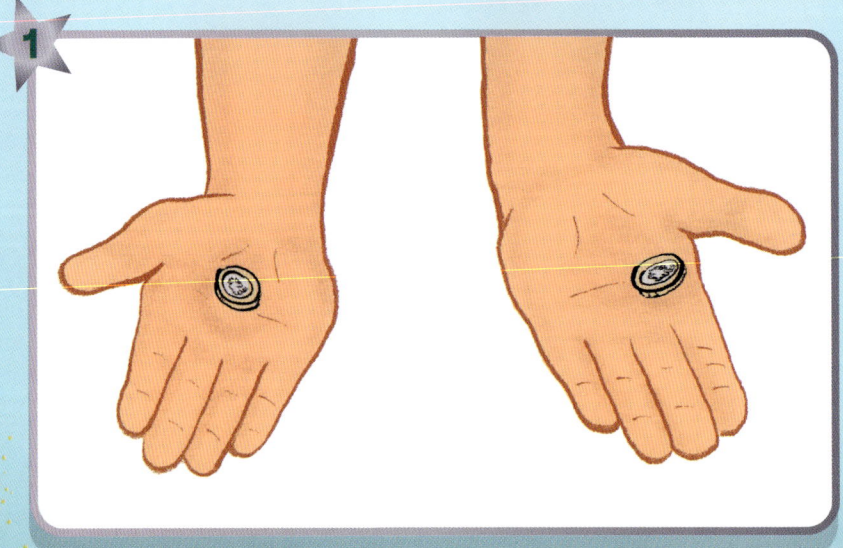

1

Place a coin in the palm of one hand and one on the inside edge of the other hand.

2

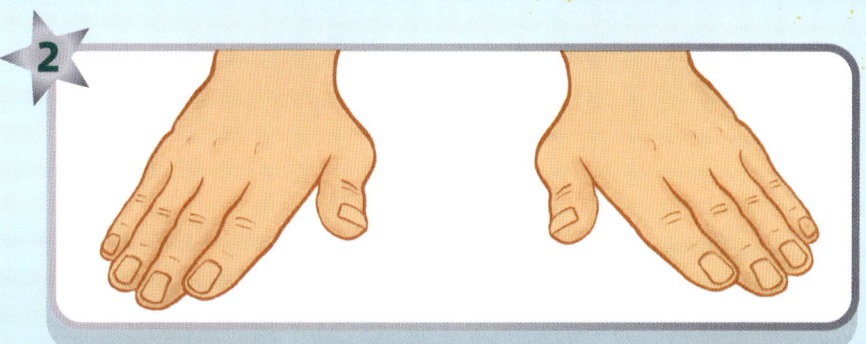

Flip both hands over onto the table, but as you flip one hand over quickly, shoot the coin across the table.

Turn your other hand over slightly more slowly so you can catch and trap both coins underneath it.

3 Fidget the fingers of your now-empty hand as if the coin is escaping.

4

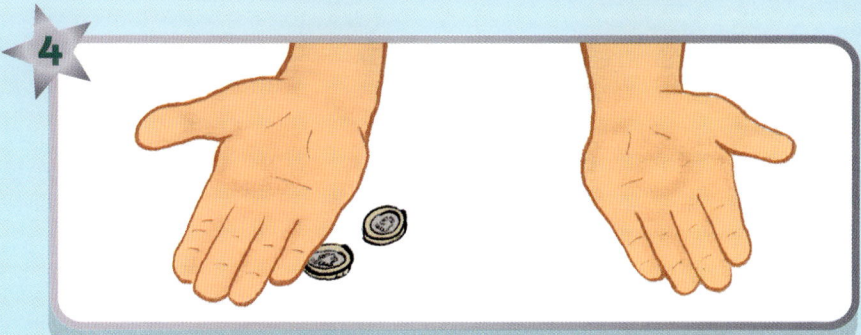

Now turn over both hands to reveal both coins sitting there.

TOP TIP Use two differently shaped coins while practising to tell where each one ends up.

DOUBLE YOUR MONEY

Who says magic doesn't pay? With some preparation and careful counting, you can turn three coins into six.

YOU WILL NEED

* Two paper plates
* Six identical coins
* Double-sided sticky tape

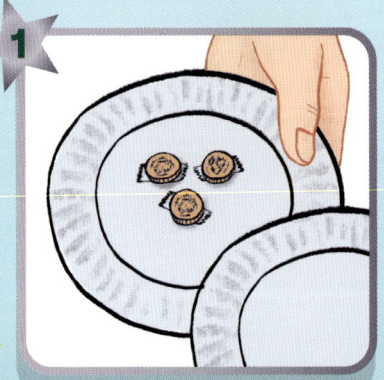

1

Before the show, use double-sided sticky tape to fasten three coins to one paper plate. Stack the empty plate on top.

2

Showtime! In front of your audience, place the three loose coins on the empty paper plate, betting that you can double the money.

3

Take the prepared plate out from underneath, tilting it away to hide the stuck coins.

4

Turn the prepared plate over like a lid on the other plate, hiding all coins.

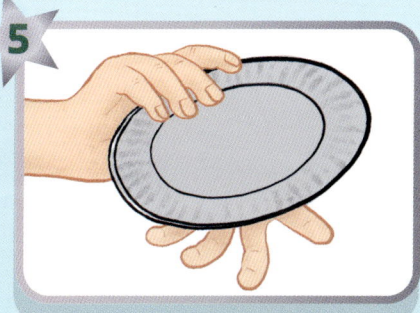

5

Holding the plates tightly together, turn them over an odd number of times.

6

Remove the top plate (which should now be the empty plate) and look: the three loose coins have fallen on the three stuck coins!

TOP TIP

You must turn the plates over once, three times, or five times! Otherwise, the stuck coins will end up still hidden in the top plate.

CHANGING FACES

Ever wished you could change
the cards you're dealt? Now you can!
With this two-faced routine *in the bag*,
you can swap your card with one shake!
You're going to need your own deck —
and not an expensive one . . .

YOU WILL NEED
* A ziplock bag
* Glue stick

1

To prepare, choose a royal and a number card. Glue them
together, back-to-back, and put them in the bag.

2 Showtime! Hold the clear bag by its top edge and show your audience the card.

3 Give the bag a shake to hide the trick.

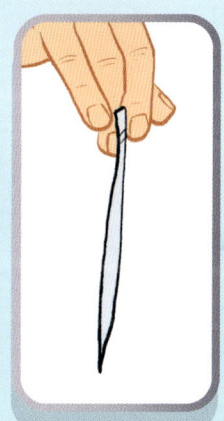

Using your middle finger, twist the bag around mid-shake.

5 Ta-da! The card has changed its face!

TOP TIP

Before showing anyone, practise twisting the bag in the mirror.

AN ACE PAIRING

In this card trick, two of the aces will 'find' the other two! If you nail the moves, the magic works without any sleight of hand . . .

YOU WILL NEED

★ A deck of playing cards

1

To prepare, hide one ace on top of the deck and another ace on the bottom. Display the other two aces face-up on the table.

2

Showtime! With a volunteer, deal cards face-down until they say 'stop'.

3

Place one of the face-up aces on top of this pile.

4

Put the cards in your hand on top of that pile. Remember the ace on the bottom? Now it's next to the face-up one!

5

With the whole pile, deal again until they say 'stop'.

6

Place the second face-up ace on top.

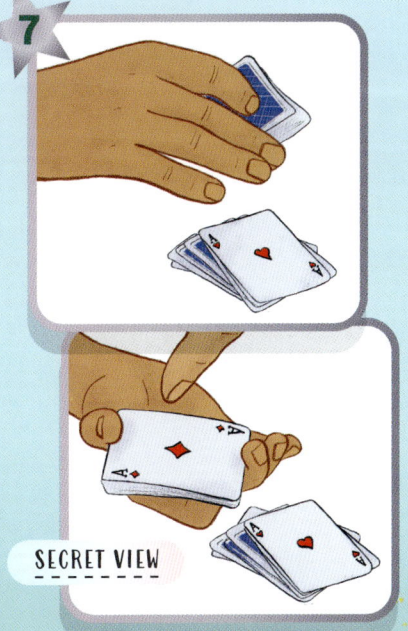

SECRET VIEW

Put the rest of the deck on top of that.

8

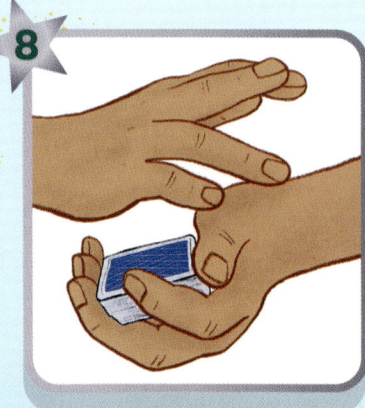

Make a magic gesture over the deck.

Spread the deck out face-down from left to right until you see the two face-up aces.

9

10

Once you know the motions, try pairing the aces by colour!

For each ace, reveal it with the card to its right: another ace. Unbelievable!

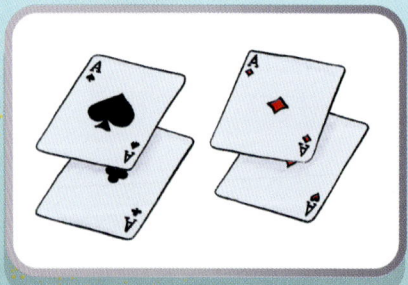

CUT THE ROPE

Great tricks can outlive their magicians, and this one's been going for a *century*. Audiences just love seeing rope get split and fixed! How's it done? You'll need a little something extra . . .

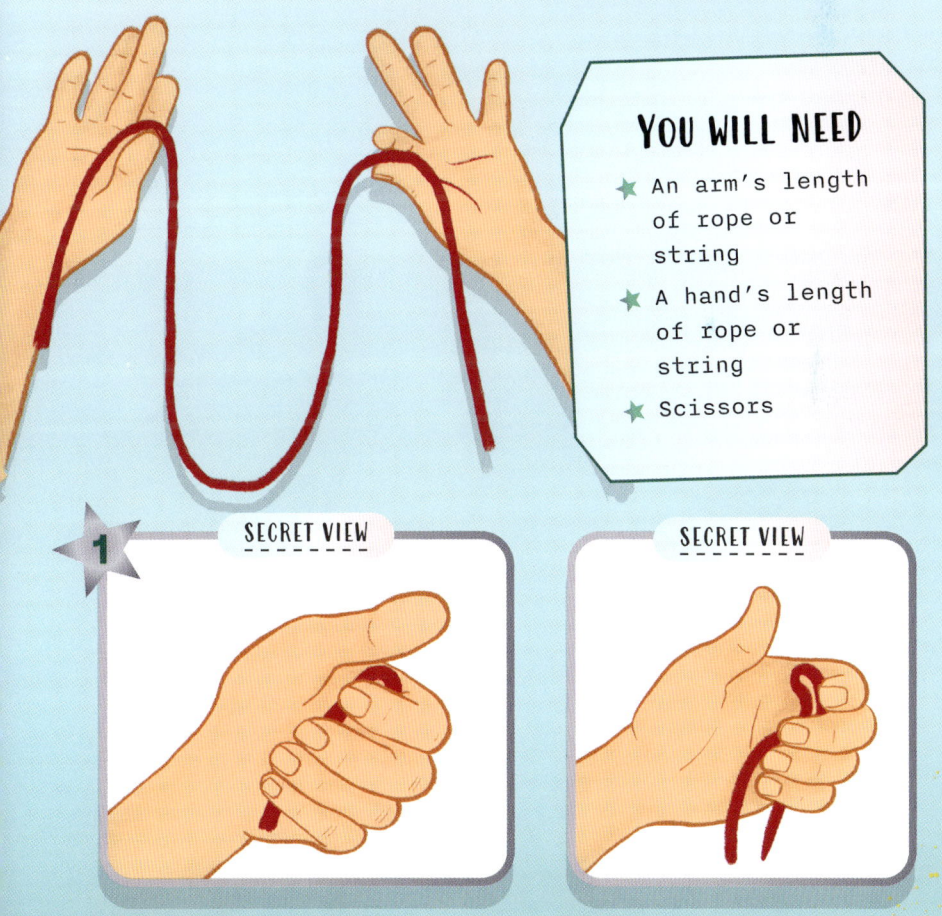

1

SECRET VIEW

SECRET VIEW

Before the performance, take the short length of rope and hide it in your hand.

Showtime! With the same hand, grip the middle of the long rope. Let both ends hang together.

Tug the loop of the short rope to poke up out of your hand.

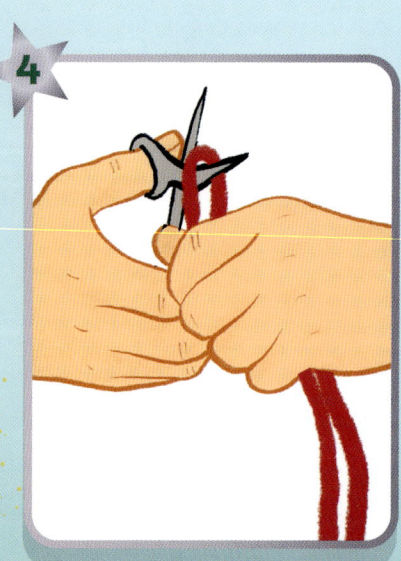

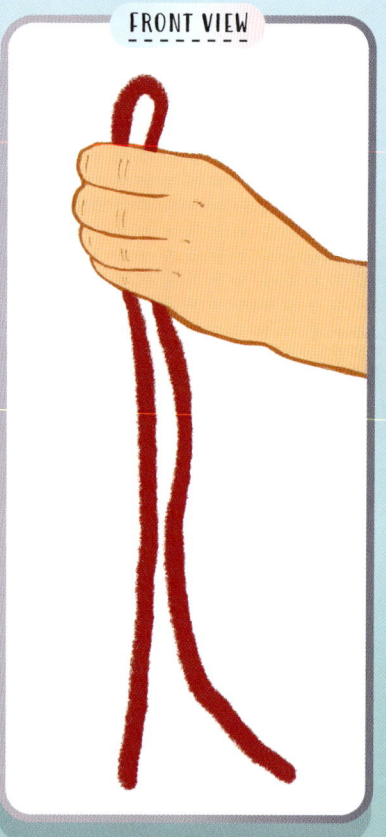

With scissors, carefully cut the loop of the short rope.

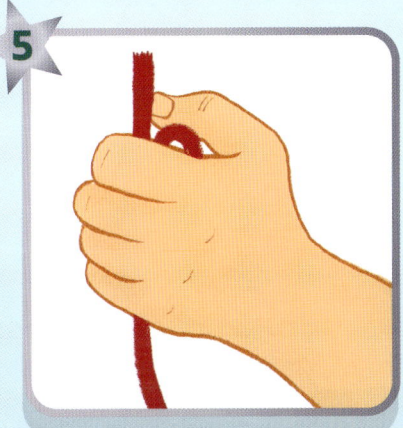

5

Claiming you will now fix it, tuck the cut ends into your fist. Magic gesture . . .

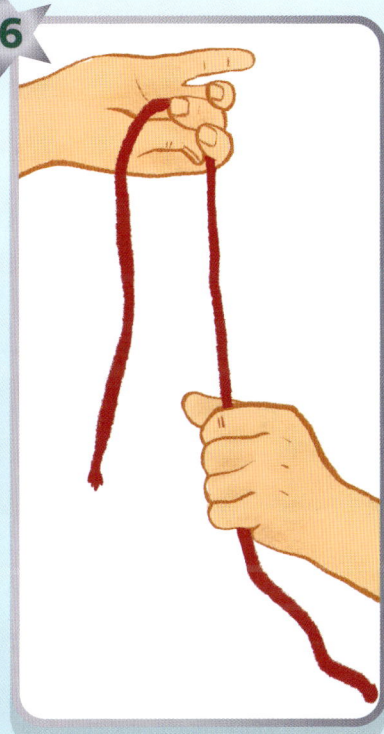

6

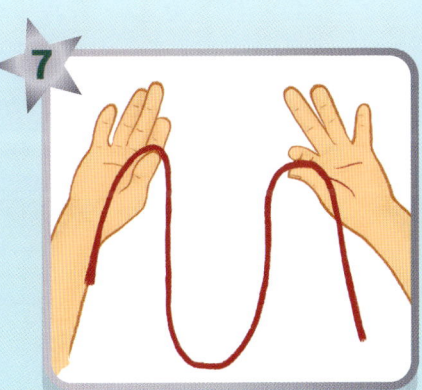

7

Dump or pocket the short pieces and show off the long rope with open hands!

With your other hand, slowly pull only the long rope out of your hand – repaired!

TOP TIP

For safety around sharp scissors, ask an adult to cut the loop. Audience participation will add that wow factor!

PAPER MONEY

Paper becomes money before your audience's eyes! Magic this impressive takes careful preparation, sticking a folded banknote perfectly to the paper. Then it's just a quick flip and unfold for a round of applause.

YOU WILL NEED

★ A banknote (get permission!)
★ A piece of paper the same size as the banknote
★ Glue stick

2

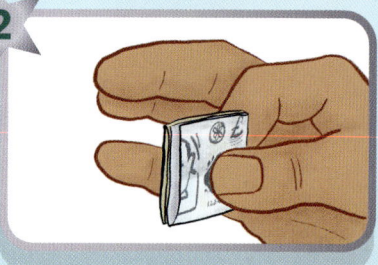

Lining up the two squares – hiding the banknote perfectly – glue them together.

1

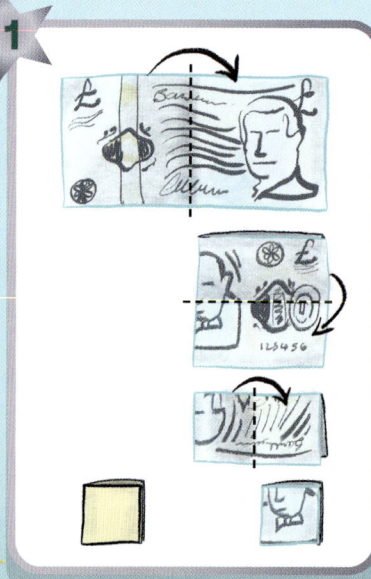

To prepare, fold the paper and the banknote three times into identical squares.

3 SECRET VIEW

When dry, unfold only the paper side.

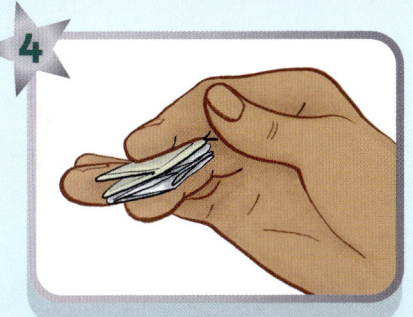

4 Showtime! Show your audience the paper side and fold it back into a square.

5 Pinching the square between your thumb and index finger, start to shake it!

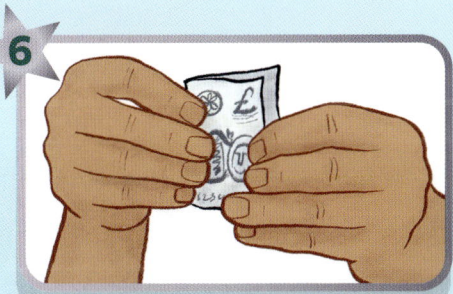

6 Mid-shake, flip it around your middle finger to face the banknote towards the audience.

7 Unfold the square to reveal the banknote fully. This reaction's *priceless*!

TOP TIP Definitely practise this with a mirror to see what they'll see – and mind their position! Crowd to the front, please . . .

THE TWO OF ACES

We've transformed a card before, but now we're doubling them too! Transforming a 2 into two aces (because aces are often worth 1) is a real, advanced test of working quickly without looking. Start slow!

YOU WILL NEED

★ 3 playing cards: two aces and a 2
★ Glue stick

1

To prepare, lightly glue the back of one ace to the back of your 2.

2

Hide the other ace facing the first one. It's a fake back for the 2 card!

3

Showtime! Show the audience the front and back of the 2. Normal, right?

4

Very quickly, pull out the loose ace with one hand, and spin the 2 in your other.

5

To your audience, the 2 has burst apart into its value: two aces!

TOP TIP

You might need a loud misdirect to hide the trick . . .

2D TO 3D

Have you always wanted to bring a picture to life? This trick will show you how to turn a 2D drawing into a 3D object — and amaze your audience! You'll need to be sitting on a chair at a table for this one.

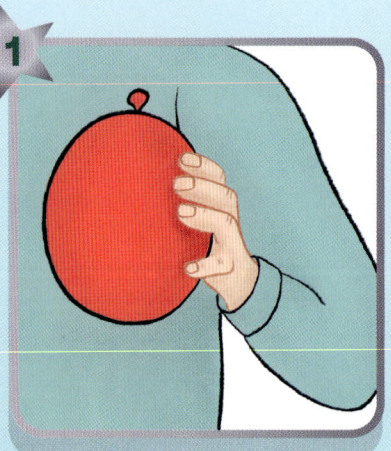

1

To prepare, blow up the balloon, tie it and rest it on your lap with the tied end pointing upwards towards the edge of the table. Make sure it's hidden from your audience.

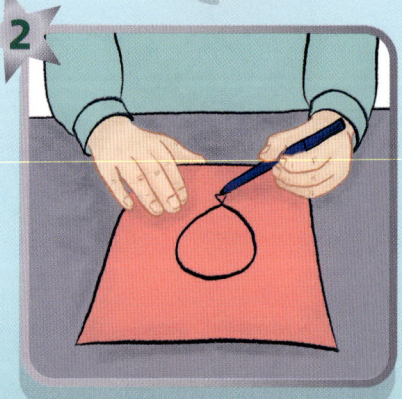

2

Showtime! Now your audience is watching, draw a big balloon on the piece of paper.

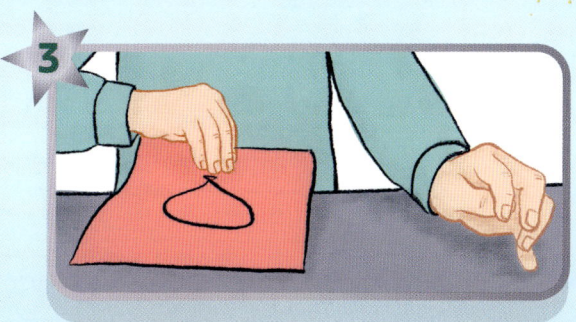

3

Pull the paper back towards the edge of the table. Use your thumb to grab hold of the balloon knot and hide the balloon behind the paper as you lift the drawing up to show your audience.

SECRET VIEW

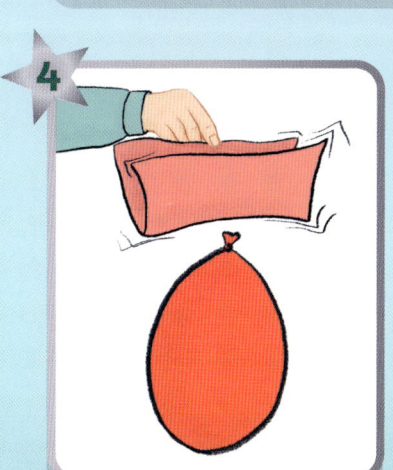

4

While the audience focuses on your picture, use your other hand to grab the balloon and push it from behind the paper to dazzle your audience.

TOP TIP

Make sure your balloon is blown up no bigger than the size of the paper!

THE ROLLING STRAW

This enchanted straw follows your finger, then rolls away all by itself! You could say the answer to this one is *blowing in the wind*, because it's actually — shhh! — just a gentle breath . . .

YOU WILL NEED

* A paper straw
* A smooth table

1

Lay the straw out horizontally.

2

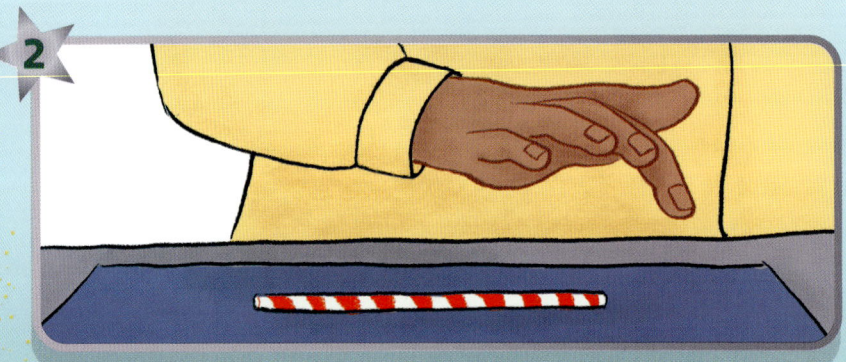

Wave your hand over the straw and explain that you will use the magic in your finger to move the straw - without touching it!

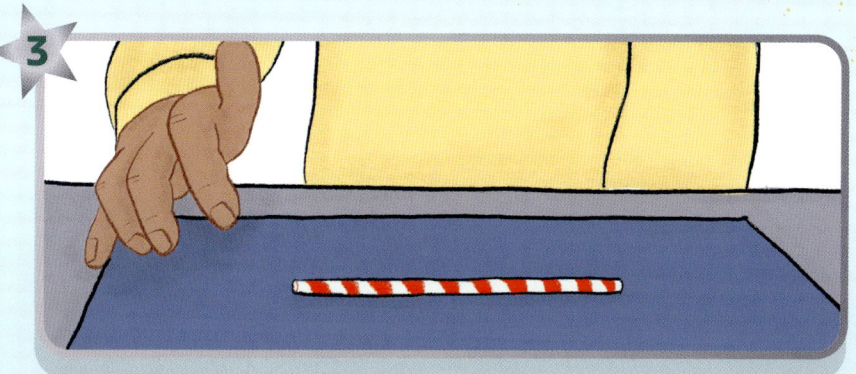

Place your finger just ahead of the straw and gently begin to blow, anticipating the path with your finger.

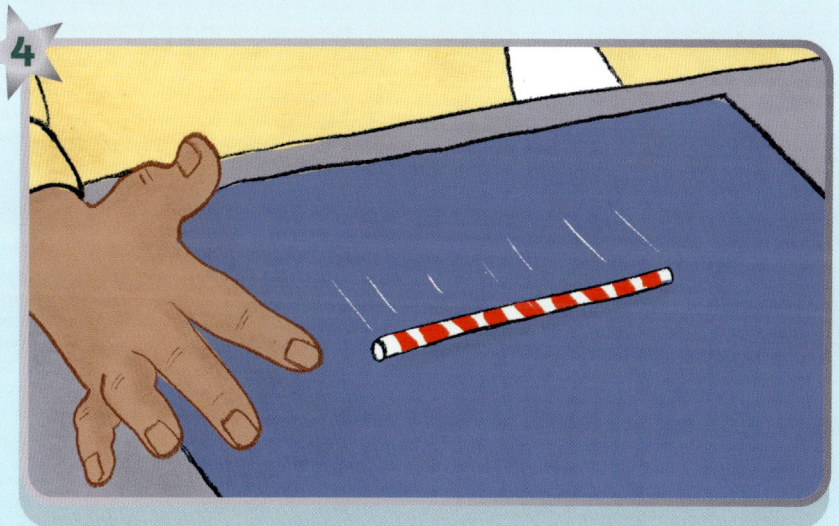

When you start to lose control, pull away your finger and let it roll!

TOP TIP

Practise controlling your breathing to move the straw at just the right pace.

THE DANCING STRAW

Wow your audience with the power of your mind as you make a straw dance . . . Actually, you'll be using a hidden finger to wiggle it around — but the effect is hilarious!

YOU WILL NEED

★ A straw
★ Sticky tape

1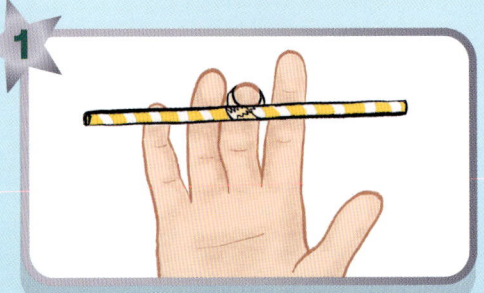

Out of sight, tape the middle of the straw to your middle finger's tip.

2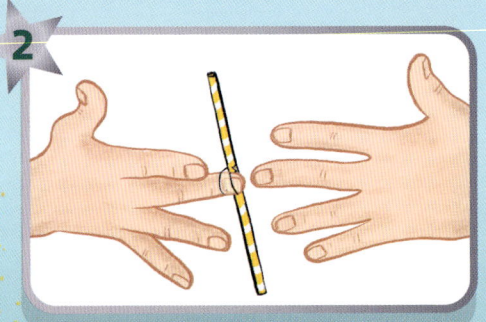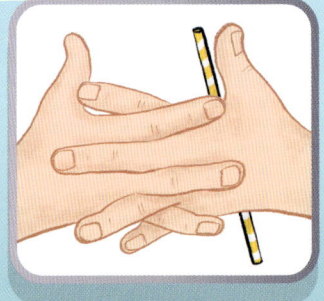

Interlace your fingers, keeping the one with the straw tucked freely inside your hands. The straw should be visible above and below the wall of your hands.

SECRET VIEW

3

Showtime! Tell your audience you're about to use the power of your mind to move the straw.

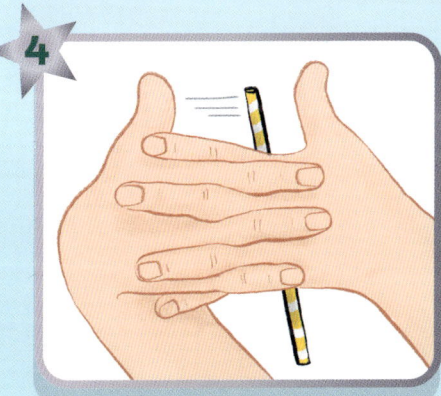

4

5

Visibly concentrate, slowly wiggling your finger. For everyone watching, the straw starts dancing!

For an ending flourish, break your hands apart and pretend to catch the straw, keeping the tape hidden. This will convince them it was always loose.

TOP TIP

Practise your magical concentrating face so it looks like you really are transmitting brain waves to the straw!

MIND–READING NUMBERS

This number trick will astound your audience with your mind-reading powers. Even better, it works every time — as long as your volunteer does their adding-up right!

YOU WILL NEED

⭐ Two pieces of paper
⭐ Pen
⭐ Envelope

To prepare, double the current year. So, if it's 2025, write 4050 nice and big on a piece of paper. Seal it in the envelope.

2 Showtime! Ask your volunteer to write down four numbers:

- The year they were born

- An important year in their life

- The number of years since that year

- What their age will be at the end of this year

3 Have them add up these numbers and write the total on another piece of paper.

4 Ask your volunteer to open the envelope. Enjoy the gasp: it's their number!

TOP TIP Make sure your pen works! Magicians come prepared.

HEARTS AND MINDS

This mind-bending trick makes you look psychic!
Even though they're choosing freely,
you know which card your volunteer will choose:
the six of hearts! Or any card you prefer . . .

To prepare, put the deck face-down. Put the six of hearts on
the top, then put nine cards on top of it, making it the tenth.

 2 Showtime! Tell your audience that you can
read their mind. Ask a volunteer to think of
any number between ten and twenty.

3

Draw the number of cards they have said, face-down.

4 Ask your volunteer to add the two digits of their number and tell you the result. For example, 13 becomes 1 + 3 = 4.

5

From the small pile, draw that number of cards back onto the deck.

6

Without looking, show them the last card, and ask if it's the six of hearts!

TOP TIP Learn your maths! Any number between ten and twenty, with its digits added, counts back to the tenth card.

FEEL THE FORCE

This technique, called *forcing*, can make your volunteer choose a particular card without realising it. It's a subtle motion, but with practice, they won't be able to resist!

1

To prepare, choose and memorise a card. Then put it face-down on top of the deck.

2

Showtime! Hold the deck face-down in your preferred hand, with your thumb on the top corner.

3

Until your volunteer says 'stop', flick through the cards with your thumb, like pages in a book.

4

With your other hand, lift the top pile of the deck away from you, letting your memorised top card slip down the back onto the lower pile.

5

Hand the lower pile to your volunteer. Ask them to pick and show their card.

6

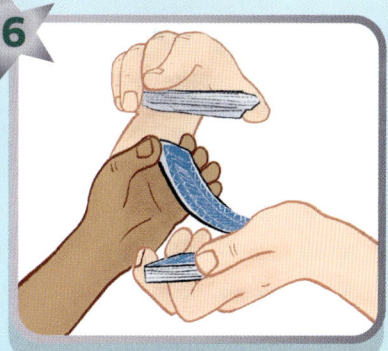

Announce your memorised card! Astounding!

If your sleight of hand is up to it, try to do the top *two* cards!

KEY CARD

This technique finds the card that your volunteer has chosen and hidden randomly. The secret is down to you remembering just one *other* card — which you're probably great at by now!

YOU WILL NEED

★ A deck of playing cards

Before you start, peek at and memorise the bottom card. That's your key card.

Showtime! Have your volunteer pick and memorise any card without showing you.

Start dealing cards onto the table, face-down, until your volunteer says 'stop'.

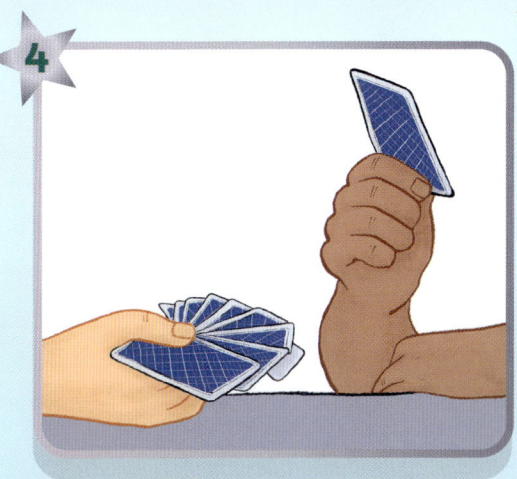

4 Ask them to put their card face-down on top of the pile.

5 Put the cards left in your hand on top of the table pile. Your key card is on top of their card!

6 Announce that you will find their card. Flip the deck face-up, find your key card, and show off the card that came before it. Ta-da!

TOP TIP For extra personality and flair, make a show of checking the cards and reading their mind, even after you know you've found it!

BEHIND YOUR BACK

This card trick seems impossible because it all happens behind your back! One sneaky move makes this an easy trick to astound your audience . . .

YOU WILL NEED

★ A deck of playing cards

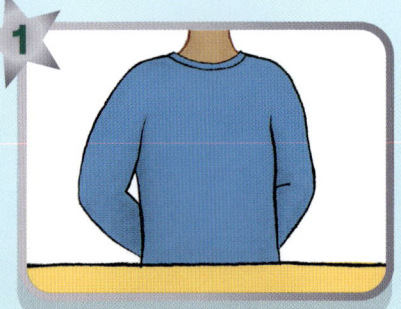

Tell your audience you'll be doing this amazing trick behind your back! Then show them how you'll be holding the deck of cards behind you.

With the cards behind your back, sneakily put the card from the top of the deck upside-down on the bottom of the deck.

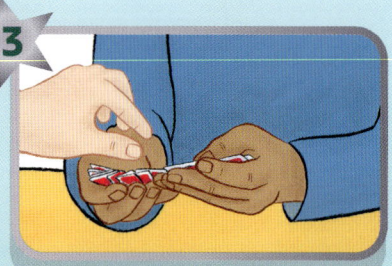

Now offer the spread of cards, face-down, for your volunteer to pick one. Remember not to show the bottom card!

While they're looking at their chosen card, flip your hand holding the deck so all the cards are face-up, apart from the one on top.

Take their card (without looking at it) and place it somewhere in the middle of the deck. Do it carefully so your audience doesn't see that the rest of the cards are all face-up.

Return the deck behind your back and tell the audience you are magically looking for their card, but actually return the sneaky card from the bottom of the deck to the top.

Spread the deck out onto a table and the chosen card will be revealed as the only one face-up!

TOP TIP

Step 1 is the most important step even though it just looks like a bit of banter to your audience!

SPELLING CARD TRICK

This is one of my favourite card tricks! You'll need to know how to write the name of the person you're performing the trick to, because it will reveal their card. Quite the magic *spell*!

1

YOU WILL NEED

★ A deck of playing cards

Ask a volunteer to shuffle the deck. When they return it, peek at the bottom card. This is your key card.

2

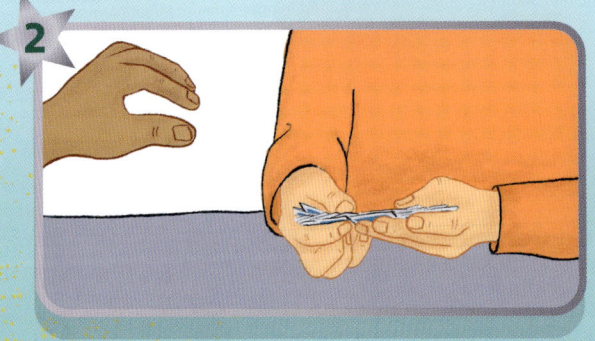

Fan the cards facing down. Ask your volunteer to show one card to the audience, but not to you.

3

Split the deck into two piles. Ask your volunteer to place their card on the pile taken from the top.

4

Place the other pile on top of their card. This puts their card under the key card!

5

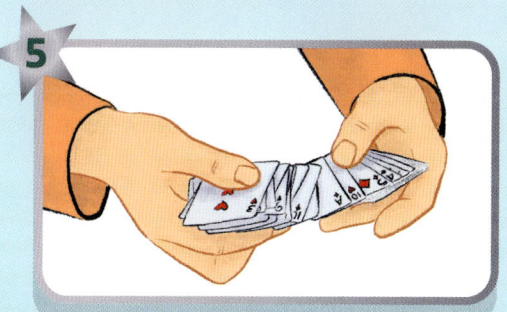

Flip the deck and search for the key card. Your volunteer's card is the one before the key card.

6

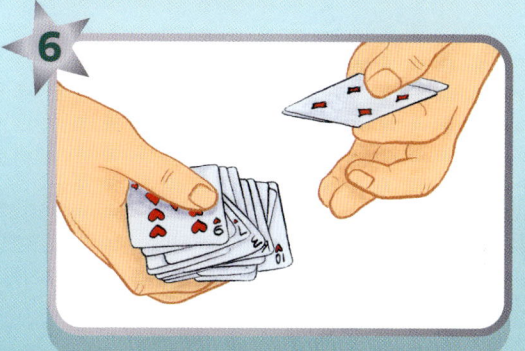

When you find it, silently count out one more card for each letter of their name, starting with the key card.

7 Keeping the deck face-up, cut it after the last card you count. Put the pile with your counted cards underneath the other pile.

8 Turn the deck face-down and ask your volunteer to spell their name. From the top, draw one card for each letter.

9 Tell them to announce their card – and then you can reveal it as the next one!

TOP TIP

When silently counting in step 6, distract your audience with patter: ask them questions to let you think!

THE PAPER EGG

Prepare to make your audience *eggs*-tremely amazed as you transform a tissue into an egg! Psst! You're actually stuffing the tissue into a complete, empty eggshell . . . Simpler, right?

YOU WILL NEED

* An egg
* A spoon
* A tissue

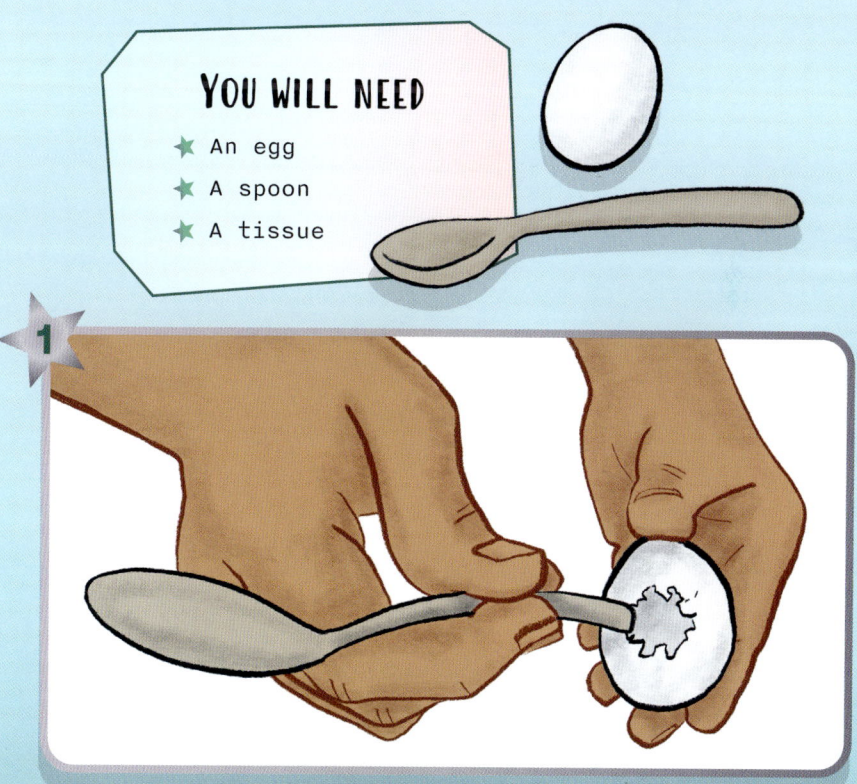

To prepare the raw egg, use the spoon to tap and peel a small hole in the shell. This will be the hidden back of the egg. Be careful not to eat any raw egg!

2

Poke through the film to wash out the eggshell. Leave to dry.

3

Showtime! Hide the egg in a loose grip with your hand at your side and flourish the tissue.

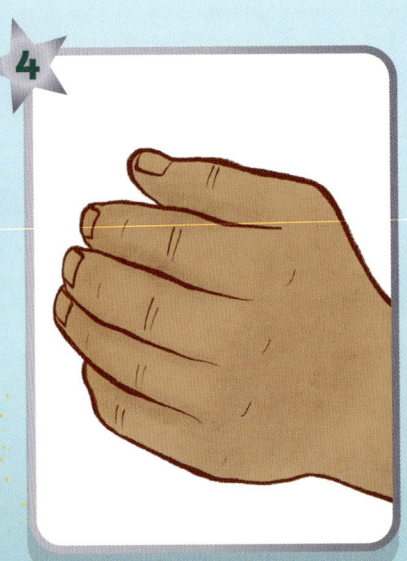

4

SECRET VIEW

Raise your egg hand, hole towards you, and gently poke the tissue inside.

5

When the tissue is packed in, make your magical gesture, and reveal the egg!

6

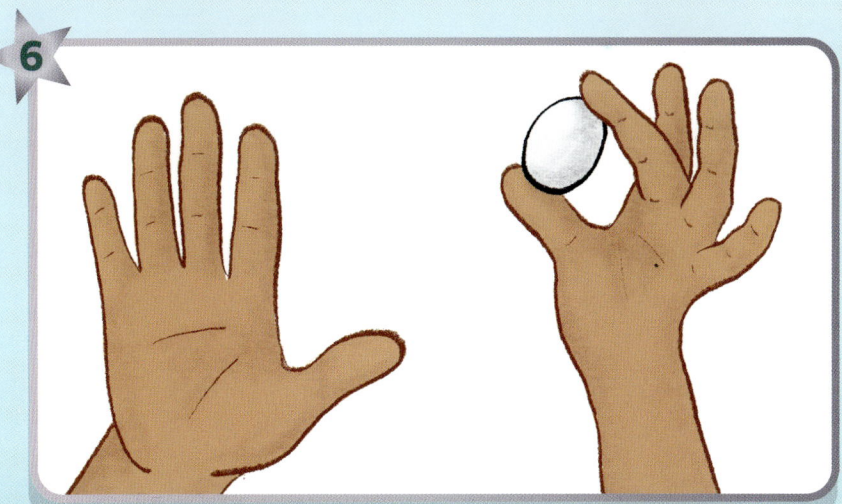

TOP TIP You could also try this with a chocolate egg!

APPEARING SILK

Ah, the humble hanky! It's a magician's best friend for a reason. This quick and easy trick summons a handkerchief out of thin air — useful for anyone with a runny nose . . .

YOU WILL NEED

- ★ An elastic band
- ★ A colourful handkerchief
- ★ Sleeves

1

To prepare, hang the handkerchief halfway through the elastic band.

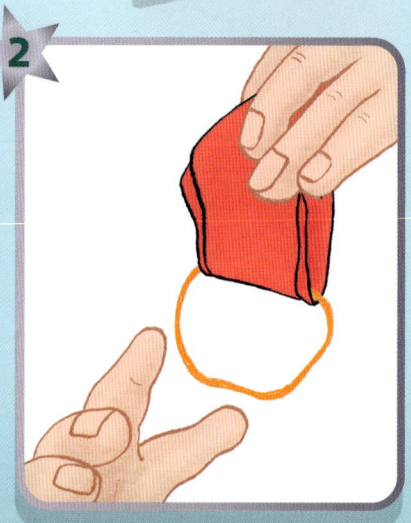

2

Fold the handkerchief nice and small, with the elastic band a relaxed loop.

3

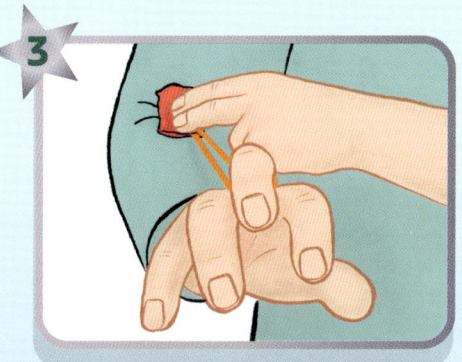

Stretch the loop from your middle finger down your sleeve, trapping the handkerchief in the crook of your arm.

4

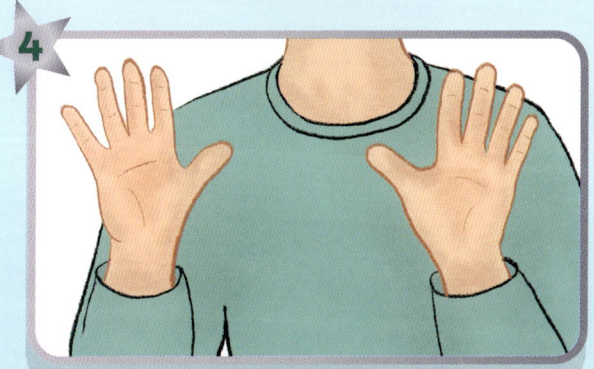

To perform, hold your hands up and open, say a magic word, and . . .

5

Try it with two hands, two arms, two handkerchiefs!

Straighten your arm! Freed, the handkerchief will ping out into your hand.

SWEET CATCH

The hand is quicker than the eye — and you can prove it. This trick will show you throwing a sweet up and catching it on one finger! Such skill! This one's a *treat* . . .

YOU WILL NEED

★ Two identical sweets, each with a hole big enough to fit on your finger

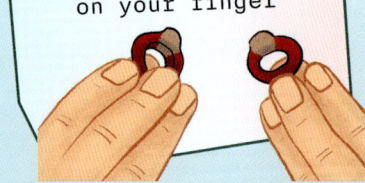

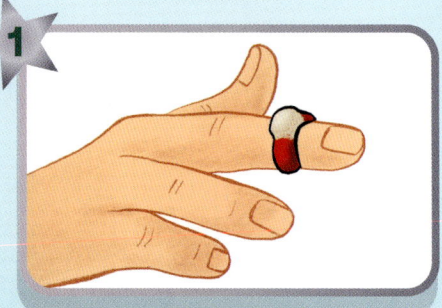

1

To prepare, put your index finger through the hole of one of the sweets. Keep this hand hidden!

2

Showtime! With your other hand, toss the second sweet into the air and catch it a few times, using your patter on the audience.

3

When they least expect it, throw the sweet again, but this time use your hidden hand to catch it.

4

SECRET VIEW

Close your fist around the sweet, but keep your index finger outstretched. The first sweet will be hidden away, but they'll think you caught it on your finger!

5

Secretly drop the caught sweet into your sleeve, pocket, or on the floor, and open your fist to show your magical powers.

TOP TIP

Timing is the trick here. Practise until you can do the throwing and the catching at the same time naturally.

OUT OF THIS WORLD

This card trick makes your *audience* magic!
Ask a volunteer to separate a deck of cards,
purely by guesswork, into piles of black or red.
Flip the cards, and reveal they've
done an almost perfect job . . .

1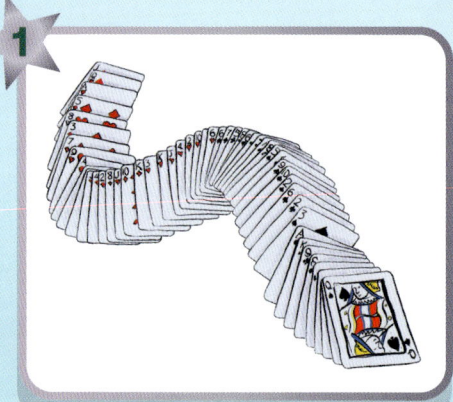

YOU WILL NEED

★ A deck of
   playing cards

To prepare, put all the
red cards on top of all the
black cards, face-down.

2

Showtime! Ask one volunteer to deal out the top half
of the deck face-down into two piles, without looking:
red on the left, black on the right.

3

When they're done, ask a second volunteer to do the same with the remaining cards – but this time, to do red cards on the right and black cards on the left.

4

Picking up one pile yourself, with a volunteer for the other, spread the cards out face-up. Both piles will be perfectly separated, half and half each!

TOP TIP Prepare some patter to keep the rest of your audience included!

Stephen Mulhern

is one of television's most in-demand presenters, with a string of smash-hit television shows including *Catchphrase, In for a Penny, You Bet!* and *Deal or No Deal*. As well as being an award-winning presenter, Stephen is one of the best magicians in TV today and is the only magician in the world to have performed on the Royal Variety Performance four times! He has performed in shows all over the country in front of some of the most recognised people in the world, including Queen Elizabeth II and, most recently, the King himself!

Scan the QR code below to see me performing some tricks and revealing all-important secrets so you can impress all your friends and family!

THANK YOU TO . . .

My Mum and Dad for all your support and love. Thank you for helping me believe in myself! Love you so much x

Jamie, Susie, Chris and Vince for everything we have achieved so far!

Claire Dundas, Paul Worsley, Emily Page and Matt Page at YMU Management.

Stephen Williams Jr for your help with the magic!

Jeni Child for designing the book and all the fantastic illustrations for the magic trick instructions.

Begoña Fernández Corbalán for the pictures of Max Magic.

Dominica Clements for the truly magical cover design.

Jenny Jacoby for bringing the book together.

Ruth Bennett for managing the project.

Sam Fern for copy-editing.

Saranne Taylor-Herbert for proofreading.

Aimee White for editorial assistance.

Alex May and Eloise Angeline
for the print production.

Kate Griffiths, Steph Bramwell-Lawes
and Bethany Copeland-Ghani for sales.

Amber Ivatt, Sarah Lough and Samara Iqbal
for publicity and marketing.

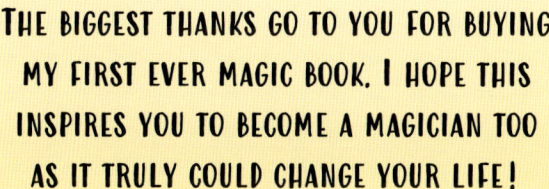

The biggest thanks go to you for buying
my first ever magic book. I hope this
inspires you to become a magician too
as it truly could change your life!

WANT MORE MAGIC?

Read Stephen Mulhern's
magical fiction series – out now!